My First Science Boo[k]

T0012143

Shapes Can Make Buildings

by Miranda Kelly

TABLE OF CONTENTS

A Crabtree Seedlings Book

CRABTREE
Publishing Company
www.crabtreebooks.com

Shapes Can Make Buildings

Look around.

Shapes are everywhere.

Shapes help us build things.

We build roofs with triangles.

Find the triangles.

We make doors
with rectangles.

We build walls
with rectangles.

Find the rectangles.

We make windows
with squares.

We build floors
with squares.

Find the squares.

We use circles too!

Glossary

 **circles** (SUR-kuhlz): Circles are shapes that are perfectly round.

 **rectangles** (REK-tang-guhlz): Rectangles have two long sides and two shorter sides.

 **squares** (SQUAIRZ): Squares are shapes that have four equal sides.

 **triangles** (TRYE-ang-guhlz): Triangles are shapes that have three sides.

Index

School-to-Home Support for Caregivers and Teachers

This book helps children grow by letting them practice reading. Here are a few guiding questions to help the reader build his or her comprehension skills. Possible answers appear here in red.

Before Reading

- **What do I think this book is about?** *I think this book is about building houses. I think this book is about shapes.*

- **What do I want to learn about this topic?** *I want to learn about different shapes. I want to learn how different shapes are used to make buildings.*

During Reading

- **I wonder why...** *I wonder why roofs are like triangles. I wonder why bricks are red.*

- **What have I learned so far?** *I have learned that walls are built with rectangles. I have learned that floors are built with squares.*

After Reading

- **Read the book again and look for the glossary words.** *I see the word **triangles** on page 6, and the word **rectangles** on page 10. The other glossary words are found on page 23.*

Library and Archives Canada Cataloguing in Publication

Title: Shapes can make buildings / by Miranda Kelly.
Names: Kelly, Miranda, 1990- author.
Description: Series statement: My first science books | "A Crabtree seedlings book". | Includes index.
Identifiers: Canadiana (print) 20210203897 |
    Canadiana (ebook) 20210203900 |
    ISBN 9781427159465 (hardcover) |
    ISBN 9781427159540 (softcover) |
    ISBN 9781427160119 (HTML) |
    ISBN 9781427160195 (EPUB) |
    ISBN 9781427160461 (read-along ebook)
Subjects: LCSH: Shapes—Juvenile literature. | LCSH: Geometry—Juvenile literature. | LCSH: Buildings—Juvenile literature.
Classification: LCC QA445.5 .K45 2022 | DDC j516/.15—dc23

Library of Congress Cataloging-in-Publication Data

Available at the Library of Congress

Crabtree Publishing Company

www.crabtreebooks.com   1–800–387–7650

Written by Miranda Kelly
Print coordinator: Katherine Berti

Print book version produced jointly with Blue Door Education in 2022

Printed in the U.S.A./062021/CG20210401

Content produced and published by Blue Door Publishing LLC dba Blue Door Education, Melbourne Beach FL USA. Copyright Blue Door Publishing LLC. All rights reserved. No part of this book may be reproduced or utilized in any form or by any means, electronic or mechanical including photocopying, recording, or by any information storage and retrieval system without permission in writing from the publisher.

Photo credits:
Shutterstock.com: Cover; hikesterson, Pg2/3; Jon Bilous. istock.com: Pg4/5; Michael Warren, Pg6/7; TT. Shutterstock.com: Pg8/9; karamysh, Pg10/11; Ruslan Kalnitsky. Pg12/13; Bogdanhoda. Shutterstock.com: Pg14/15; Brian Goodman. i-stock.com: Pg 16/17; Ratth, Pg18/19; wabeno, Pg20/21; flammulated, Pg22/23; amoklv/shutterstock.com

Published in the United States
Crabtree Publishing
347 Fifth Ave.
Suite 1402-145
New York, NY 10016

Published in Canada
Crabtree Publishing
616 Welland Ave.
St. Catharines, Ontario
L2M 5V6